EPHESIANS

Made Complete in Christ

Stonecroft

where she is ✝ as she is

Designed and Typeset by Serena Lilli Jeanne

Written by Janice Mayo Mathers

ISBN: 978-0-9908500-3-8

Produced and Distributed by:

Stonecroft
10561 Barkley Suite 500
Overland Park, KS 66212

800.525.8627 / connections@stonecroft.org

www.stonecroft.org

1216

Table of Contents

Acknowledgments

We acknowledge and thank Janice Mayo Mathers for her dedication in serving the Lord through Stonecroft. Speaker, author, and member of the Board of Directors, Jan is the author of Ephesians: Made Complete in Christ. We appreciate her love for God's Word and her love for people who need Him.

Special thanks goes to the team who prayed for Jan, and those who edited, designed, and offered their creative input to make Stonecroft Bible Studies accessible to all.

Welcome to Stonecroft Bible Studies!

It doesn't matter where you've been or what you've done — God wants to be in relationship with you. And one place He tells you about Himself is in His Word: the Bible. Whether the Bible is familiar or new to you, its contents will transform your life and bring answers to your biggest questions.

Gather with people in your communities — women, men, couples, young and old alike — and consider the message of Ephesians. Reflect on the big love of God and find the strength and power He provides to live victoriously.

Each chapter on Ephesians includes discussion questions to stimulate meaningful conversation, specific Scripture verses to investigate, and time for prayer to connect with God and each other.

Discover more of God and His ways through this small-group exploration of the Bible.

Tips for Using This Study

This book includes several features that make it easy to use and helpful for your life:

- The page number or numbers given after every Bible reference are keyed to the page numbers in the Abundant Life Bible. This paperback Bible uses the New Living Translation, a translation in straightforward, up-to-date language. We encourage you to obtain a copy through your group leader or at stonecroft.org.

- Each chapter ends with a section called "Thoughts, Notes, and Prayer Requests." Use this space for notes or for thoughts that come to you during your group time or study, as well as prayer requests.

- Please make this book and study your own. We encourage you to use it and mark it in any way that helps you grow in your relationship with God.

If you find this study helpful, you may want to investigate other resources from Stonecroft. Please take a look at Stonecroft "Resources" in the back of the book or online at stonecroft.org/store.

INTRODUCTION

L ove overcomes. When we unite as one in God's family, we are an unstoppable force. In Ephesians we find the power of unity in diversity and keys for healthy, satisfying relationships. This book vividly explains the life-changing magnitude of God's love and provision for you in the daily battles you face.

Paul wrote the book of Ephesians as a letter to the church at Ephesus sometime between 60 and 65 AD. Its impact on readers through the centuries is immeasurable. As you read Ephesians, you may be captivated by Paul's effusive language. What makes his joy so remarkable is that Paul was in prison when he wrote this letter. But then Paul was an unusual man with an amazing story.

When we first read about Paul in the Bible, he is called Saul. He was an influential, devout Jewish man who belonged to a strict religious group known as Pharisees who did not believe Jesus was the Son of God. In fact, Saul put considerable effort into harassing anyone who dared to believe in Jesus. He used his position of influence to have Christ-followers arrested, beaten, and sometimes even executed.

One day on his way from Jerusalem to Damascus, while searching for more believers to imprison, Saul experienced a transformational encounter with Jesus which changed his identity. The light of God struck Saul who went blind and had to be led the rest of the way to Damascus. For three days he remained blind and so distressed he neither ate nor drank. Then God sent a man named Ananias to pray for him. Saul's physical sight was restored, and he gained brand new spiritual sight as well. From that moment on he understood who Jesus is — the Son of God who died for his sins.

His immediate transformation compelled him to become as avid in his commitment to Jesus Christ and His followers as he had been against them. Until the day he was martyred for his faith, Paul never stopped telling people about Jesus Christ and His love. Eventually, God called Saul to tell the Gentiles — non Jews — about Jesus. From that point on, Saul was called Paul, his Greek name. He now had a new name to go with his new identity. And he was compelled: "We cannot stop telling about everything we have seen and heard," he said (Acts 4:20, p. 833). "Christ's love controls us" (2 Corinthians 5:14, page 884).

Prior to writing Ephesians, Paul taught and preached in Jerusalem. There, some fellow Jews again accused him of heresy and treason for following Jesus. A riot ensued, with people demanding his death. When Paul appealed to Caesar based on his Roman citizenship, the authorities happily passed him along to Rome to stand trial there.

It was a lengthy, circuitous route to Rome, involving a harrowing ship-wreck and a three-month detour on the island of Malta as Paul and his fellow travelers waited for another ship to come along. Paul took full advantage of each delay and detour. Every time he was given a chance to speak to a different authority, every time he was chained to a new guard, he took the opportunity to tell them about his life-changing experience with Jesus Christ.

When Paul eventually arrived in Rome, Caesar placed him under house arrest. This was not Paul's first imprisonment and wouldn't be his last. He remained in Rome for two years, an endless series of guards watching over him as he awaited trial. Always hanging over him was the possibility of execution at the hands of the Romans known for cruelty.

In the face of his persecution, Paul wore the "armor of God" he describes in the last chapter of Ephesians. He understood that our battles in this life are not with flesh and blood, but with Satan — an adversary we can't see whose attacks we experience often as believers. And he knew that his brothers and sisters in Christ were essential to his victorious, faith-filled perseverance.

That Paul was able to write this encouraging, joy-filled letter during such a trying time speaks to the powerful reality of God's overcoming love. He related to God as a son and heir through Christ (Galatians 4:5-7) and as one accepted in the Beloved (Ephesians 1:6).

Like Paul's transformational journey with Jesus Christ, we hope you, too, will experience lasting change by encountering God's love in the book of Ephesians. As you spend time reflecting on the lengths to which He goes to express His love may you discover the strength and power to walk victorious through every battle.

Enjoy!

– Stonecroft

chapter 1

POWER FOR THOSE
WHO BELIEVE

"S NO-O-O-O-W!"

My friend heard her four-year-old son's excited shout from his upstairs bedroom after waking to the sight of winter blanketing the landscape outside his window. She heard him racing around in his room then clomping down the stairs.

"I'm ready to go play in the snow!" he announced.

She turned to see him standing there stark naked — except for snow boots. She decided to see just how far he'd go with this and followed him to the door. As he stepped outside, a rush of frigid air whooshed around him.

"Whoa!" he said, ducking back inside. "I need a hat."

How often have you felt yourself unprepared to face what life delivers to your door? I think it's a feeling we're all familiar with. This is why Ephesians is such an important book. It provides you with everything you need to be fully prepared for whatever life brings your way — from challenging circumstances to challenging relationships. This book offers all the tools necessary to meet life head on, joyfully and successfully.

The wonderful truth we'll discover in this study is we don't have to be strong in ourselves. We don't have to grit our teeth and tough it out. We don't need fit bodies, high IQs, or emotional fortitude. We just need God. As members of His family, He provides everything it takes to stand strong in Him and in His mighty power (Ephesians 6:10). We have the assurance Jesus is "far above any ruler or authority or power" in every battle we face. (Ephesians 1:21).

In the last chapter of Ephesians, Paul describes the "armor of God" that enabled him to experience joy throughout his extreme circumstances.

> Be strong in the Lord and in his mighty power. Put on all of God's armor so that you will be able to stand firm against all strategies of the devil. For we are not fighting against flesh-and-blood enemies, but against evil rulers and authorities of the unseen world, against mighty powers in this dark world, and against evil spirits in the heavenly places. Therefore, put on every piece of God's armor so you will be able to resist the enemy in the time of evil.
>
> – Ephesians 6:10-13 (page 898)

Did you notice the beginning phrase, *be strong in the Lord?* Paul uses this phrase seven times in the book of Ephesians to emphasize the significance and power that comes from being in Christ. And he uses the phrase *in Christ* more than fifteen times. It's a key theme of Paul's theology. If you are in Christ, you are "one" with Jesus, like the tightest of relationships. If you are in Christ, you receive all the spiritual blessings He offers. If you are in Christ, Jesus' strength is 100 percent available to you. It is impossible for you to need more than Christ is able to provide.

What does verse 11 tell us to do, and why?

15

We can go through our day only partially covered, but God's full strength is accessed when we clothe ourselves in the whole armor. No soldier would willingly go into battle partially armed. He would never risk the vulnerability. The same is true with the armor of God — anything less than the whole armor leaves us exposed and vulnerable.

To think about the armor of God helping us to stand firm, let's picture a tree. The pieces of God's armor represent all that keeps us rooted in Christ: truth, righteousness, peace, faith, salvation, and the Word of God. Through this root system, by donning God's armor, we are able to grow and flourish, forming a sturdy, indestructible trunk which represents completeness in Christ. All we need is in Him. And because we are complete, the branches of our lives — our many relationships — grow healthy and fruitful.

Just as a soldier would never go into battle alone, we are strengthened through unity with other believers. The church is Christ's body, made full and complete by Him (Ephesians 1:23, page 895). We need each other to overcome our daily battles.

God's armor equips us to fight a spiritual enemy who attacks our minds, vies for our attention, tries to control our attitude, destroys our confidence, disrupts our relationships, and steals our peace of mind. This cruel and relentless enemy attempts to deceive us into passivity, boredom, discontent, hopelessness, despair, hatred — endless sabotage designed to prevent us from living life with God and others as He designed. This conflict requires our daily vigilance. Fortunately, you don't have to design and create your own protection — God has already taken care of that! Let's look at the specific pieces of armor available to us.

Read Ephesians 6:13-17 (page 898). List the six pieces of armor described.

The armor metaphor is used by Paul to communicate the way in which we are equipped in Christ. Paul was a student of Scripture, and he may have been calling to mind the exact phrasing in Isaiah describing God putting on His own armor. "He put on righteousness like a breastplate, and a helmet of salvation on His head" (Isaiah 59:17, NASB). The armor of God we are to put on is God's and is ours in Christ Jesus.[1] He designed it with us in mind. He knows the battles we face and He left nothing to chance. In Christ Jesus we are fully equipped for anything!

Paul was a Roman citizen and a prisoner of Rome. As such he would have been familiar with the armor of a Roman soldier — from head to toe. He may have been thinking of that armor as he wrote Ephesians 6. The whole set of armor inspired awe. Each intricately designed piece protected a different part of the soldier's body. In each lesson of this study we'll look at a specific piece of armor and its applicability to following Christ in community with others.

Let's start with the helmet of salvation.

A Roman soldier's helmet, made of bronze, was so strong nothing could pierce it, not even a battle-axe. Specially designed pieces attached to the helmet protected the soldier's cheeks and jaws. Each helmet, a work of art, exhibited engraved, ornate designs.[2]

"Put on salvation as your helmet," Paul tells us in verse 17. The enemy attacks our thoughts, and when we agree with God about who He is and our redemption in Him, He begins to daily transform us through the renewing of our mind (Romans 12:2, page 866). Keep this image of the Roman helmet in your mind as we flip back to the first chapter of Ephesians where Paul beautifully describes the gift of salvation.

Read Ephesians 1:3-8 (page 895) and list what this passage says God has done for us:

He chose us! He redeemed us! We're part of His eternal family. What thoughts come to your mind as you look at this list?

Does it astound you to realize God loved you and made a plan for your life even before He created the world? What do the following verses say about this?
Ephesians 2:10 (page 896)

Psalm 139:16 (page 476)

According to Ephesians 1:5 (page 895), why has God done all of this?

Think of it! It was God's pleasure to bring you into His family and arm you with His overcoming love and power. Even before He laid the foundations of the universe, He imagined us. He made a plan that included the means by which we, the created, could enter into a relationship with Him, the Creator. This salvation, God's magnificent plan, provides the means for us to escape the deadly consequences of our sin. What is sin? It's that tendency to go our own way, do our own thing, ignore God. Broken relationships result when we decide not to do things God's way. We know that we sin because we get unreasonably angry or jealous or hurt. Sin requires punishment, but Jesus, God's Son, took the consequences of our sin upon Himself. He died so we may not suffer eternal separation from God, death that lasts forever. What sets Jesus Christ apart, what proves He is God, is that three days after His crucifixion He rose from the grave. Jesus died for our sins, loves us, and wants to live forever with us.

Read the following verses and note what they say about salvation.
John 3:16 (page 811)

Romans 6:23 (page 861)

Romans 5:8 (page 860)

Romans 10:9-10 (page 864)

God wanted more for us than just to know Him. He wanted us to partake in all that it means to be His child. According to the following verses, what else has God done for us?

Romans 8:15-17 (page 862)

John 1:12 (page 809)

Galatians 4:5 (page 892)

When we make the decision to believe Jesus Christ is the Son of God who died for our sins and ask Him for forgiveness, God sees us as His child. We are joint heirs with His only Son, Jesus Christ. We don't deserve it; we cannot earn it. God put it all in motion before even creating the world, and we were part of that plan!

Now read Ephesians 1:9-11 (page 895). What does this passage tell us about God's end goal?

Clearly, God has a master plan. Not only is it a good plan, but He has the ability and power to make everything work out according to His plan. At the center is Jesus Christ who bridges the gap between the kingdom of heaven and life on earth. There will come a time when every knee will bow and every tongue will confess that Jesus is Lord, to the glory of God the Father (Philippians 2:10-11, page 900). Even now, we have the privilege of showing God's glory to the world through our lives!

God commissioned Paul to take the message of salvation to the Gentiles as well as the Jews (Galatians 2:7). During the time Ephesians was written, there was a great spiritual and cultural divide between Jews and Gentiles. God chose Paul, a Jewish man who'd been fanatical in his hatred of Christ and His followers, to preach the message of love and unity based in Jesus Christ. Who better to do so than a man who'd been radically transformed by God's love? He was now just as fanatical about seeing others transformed.

Read Ephesians 1:12-14 (page 895). What does verse 13 say happens when we believe in Christ?

How does it say He identifies us as His own?

Something happens at the point of salvation that transforms us. When the Holy Spirit comes to live within us, He changes the way we think, feel, and behave — He changes our hearts!

Read 2 Corinthians 5:17 (page 884).

The Message paraphrase puts it this way: "The old life is gone; a new life burgeons!" The Holy Spirit living within us makes it difficult to act and think the way we did prior to our salvation. Noticeable change occurs — which brings us back to the soldiers' helmets.

> When the enemy's blow comes to our head intending to destroy (cancer diagnosis, adultery...rejection, bankruptcy, fire loss, death of a child), the helmet of salvation is what enables courageous action with the battle cry, "God has not destined me, his blood-bought saint for wrath but for obtaining salvation through our Lord Jesus Christ." Our mind must be reached with the truth that although I may be struck in battle, Christ has won the victory and in Him I will never be separated from God's love.[3]

Just as the helmet protects the soldier's head, so God designed His salvation to protect our minds. The Spirit protects our thoughts and our attitudes, which results in changed behavior. Once we put on the helmet of salvation, the world around us begins to look different.

The last part of Ephesians 1 shows us a beautiful prayer Paul prayed for his fellow Christ-followers — a prayer still very relevant to us today.

Read verses 15-23 (page 895). What are three key things Paul asks of God?

Can you think of a better series of gifts such as wisdom, revelation, and enlightenment in regard to your hope in God? What are your thoughts about these three requests? How are they relevant to your needs today?

Imagine the effect it would have on you and those around you if this became a prayer you prayed regularly. You might consider writing a personalized version of Paul's prayer on a notecard and begin each day by praying through it.

Now look at how Paul described God in verse 21 (page 895) and jot down your observations.

He is not just above evil powers. He is far above! And not only now, but for all time. This is the God who loves you and sacrificed His only Son in order to have an intimate transforming relationship with you through His incredible gift of salvation. Take a moment and let that truth settle down into you, saturating your inmost being. Ask God to open your mind to this astonishing reality. Then put on your helmet of salvation that proclaims you are a child of God.

Closing Prayer

Father, create in me a clean heart and transform me through the renewing of my mind. Give me spiritual wisdom and insight so I can grow in my knowledge of You. Flood my heart with light so I can understand the confident hope that is mine because of my salvation. Help me to understand the incredible greatness of your power that is available to me so that as a new creation in Christ Jesus I can grow in my knowledge of You, my Creator, and become more like You (Psalm 51:10, page 436; Romans 12:2, page 866; Ephesians 1:17-19, page 895; Colossians 3:10, page 903).

Personal Reflection and Application

I see

I believe

I will

Thoughts, Notes, and Prayer Requests

Healing

—— *chapter 2* ——

RECONCILED
THROUGH CHRIST

During his sophomore year of college, Steve decided to pray for the salvation of every guy on his dorm floor. Everyday. By name. With 20 rooms plus the floor supervisor, that meant praying for 40 people. Often the only time he could pray without his roommate being there was at lunch. So he gave up his lunch. He would start praying for his roommate T.J. and then work his way around the floor. As he got to know the guys better, Steve's prayers became more personal. There was one room in particular that stuck out in his prayers — 315 next to the elevators.

That was Don and Jeff's room. I wonder if it is even worth praying for them, Steve sometimes thought. There is a party in that room most every night. These guys have no interest in anything spiritual, much less Jesus. Yet he stuck to his commitment to pray for every guy on the floor, every day, by name. So, after he prayed for Matt and Dominick, Steve prayed for Don and Jeff in 315. Everyday.

First semester came to a close and the dorm emptied out for Christmas break. When he returned, Steve continued his practice of praying for every guy on his floor. A Scripture verse came to mind: "But God showed his great love for us by sending Christ to die for us while we were still sinners" (Romans 5:8).

Then one day in February, there was a knock at his door. "Steve, you're known as a religious guy," Jeff said. "I have some questions about the Bible."

Soon Jeff was attending weekly Bible studies with Steve. After a few weeks, Jeff began to understand who Jesus is and asked Him to be his Savior and Lord.

This is what it means to be reconciled through Christ (Romans 5:11, page 860).

But God... Those two tiny words are among the most wonderful words in the English language. You will find examples sprinkled throughout the entire Bible summing up what God is about: salvation, mercy, intervention, hope, life! Every instance is a demonstration of God's power and sovereignty. One occurrence of this marvelous phrase is found in Ephesians 2.

Ephesians 2:1-5

Read verses 1-5 (page 895).

Once we were dead, but God gave us life! What does verse 4 say?

Because of His great love for us, God, who is also Rich in mercy, made us alive ē Christ even when we were dead in transgressions — It is by grace you have been saved.

→ "give away" our children →

God's enormous love for us compelled Him to give His only Son to be lifted up on the cross so that whoever believes in Him will have eternal life (John 3:14-16, page 942). He provided the means for eternal life before we even cared about it, knew of its possibility, or believed in it (1 Peter 1:20, page 934). He provided for our life while we were still dead in our sinful nature (Romans 5:8). He intervened on our behalf, knowing that many would reject that intervention.

Read these passages:

Matthew 19:26 (page 750) *... but ē God all things are possible*
Romans 6:23 (page 861) *for the wages of sin is death, but gift of God eternal life*
Psalm 73:23 (page 446) *I am always ē you; you hold me by my Rt. hand*
Nehemiah 9:17 (page 378) *... You are a forgiving God, gracious, Compassionate; slow ē anger + abounding in love.*
Genesis 50:20 (page 43) *... You intended to harm me, but God intended it for good*

What words do you see repeated about God? What thoughts do these verses generate in your mind about Him?

loving, faithful —

Which verse speaks to you the most? Why?

Ps. 73:23 ... you hold me by my Rt. hand —

"My mom" !!

The Bible repeatedly describes God as merciful, loving, in control. Now let's read Ephesians 2:8-10 (page 896). According to this passage, what isn't salvation?

Not by works — it is the gift of God

Salvation is God's free gift to us — given purely by His grace. Good behavior, moral living, philanthropy, being baptized, attending church, or any action we take will not produce salvation. God does not wait for us to earn salvation. He offers it as a gift in extreme love.

How does Paul describe us in verse 10?

We are God's workmanship !! created in Christ Jesus to do good works which God prepared in advance for us to do.

"a piece of work"!

Have you ever considered yourself to be a work of art? A masterpiece no less! And yet this is exactly what we are to God. The process of making us into a masterpiece begins when we are created in Christ Jesus. Think of it! Almighty God, the Creator of this vast, magnificently intricate, precisely designed universe, is in the process of "painting His likeness on the canvas of our lives."

"We all, with unveiled face, beholding as in a mirror the glory of the Lord, are being transformed into the same image from glory to glory" (2 Corinthians 3:18, NASB).

If only for one second we could stop seeing ourselves from our own distorted perspective and truly see ourselves through God's eyes — what a difference it would make in how we live! God knows our faults and insecurities and still loves us!

Even as we were living in opposition to Him, marring His work, He saw our potential. When we appeared ruined beyond repair, He created us anew through the death of His Son, Jesus. "He made Him who knew no sin to be sin on our behalf, so that we might become the righteousness of God in Him" (2 Corinthians 5:21, NAS).

According to Ephesians 2:10, page 896, why did God create us to be His masterpiece in Christ?

"to do good works"

Our purpose goes much further than reflecting God's beauty. God created us for doing good things. God wants us to live out His love to everyone around us. This brings us to the next piece of armor: the breastplate of righteousness.

The breastplate of a Roman soldier displayed the most striking part of all the armor pieces. Made of elaborately engraved brass or bronze, the breastplate protected a soldier front and back, from the top of his neck all the way to his knees. It consisted of two pieces of metal connected by solid brass rings at the shoulders and could weigh more than 40 pounds. It guarded the soldier's heart, which Proverbs 4:23 (page 483) says "determines the course of life."

Many breastplates were covered with small, scale-like pieces of metal and the more these pieces rubbed together, the shinier they became. Imagine the sight of a fully armed soldier, standing in the sun. Now imagine thousands of them. The sight would be blinding! The more a soldier walked around in his armor, the shinier it became. Its constant use increased its brilliance.[1]

No wonder the breastplate symbolizes the righteousness we have through Jesus Christ. His righteousness completely surrounds, protects, and sustains us. The more we reflect His righteousness to the world around us, the more striking we become. His righteousness in us compels us to exhibit what to the world are illogical responses to life circumstances. Our response to success, attention, and rewards avoids an inflated ego and demonstrates humility. Our response to shattering experiences shows an increased dependence on God, rather than hopeless despair or bitterness. As His righteousness shines through, our luster increases.

In addition, our ability to navigate difficult human relationships draws attention to the power of God working within us. The message Christ preached while on Earth was not just about unity with God, it was about living in unity with our fellow man. Both were new paradigms.

Read Ephesians 2:11-18 (page 896).

The cultural divide between Jews and Gentiles was an impenetrable barrier. Jews saw Gentiles as depraved and godless. Gentiles resented the Jews' attitude of superiority.

Read verses 13 and 14 and imagine how both cultures reacted when Paul preached to them about unity. How might you have reacted?

_Q -_
Need to Re-evaluate my prior thinking -
eg. "need Nigerian ears" -

God who is love came in the flesh and fulfilled the law for His chosen Jewish people. Then He took His love one step further and "grafted" Gentile believers into this new covenant in Christ so we could all be part of His family. (See Romans 11:11-24, page 865). We were without hope until the blood of Jesus "broke down the wall of hostility" and "made peace between Jews and Gentiles by creating in Himself one new people from the two" (Ephesians 2:14-15, page 896).

Today cultures around the world are still marred by prejudice, spawning inexcusable behavior. However, as followers of Jesus wearing the breastplate of righteousness, we can overcome humanity's natural bent toward division through an attitude of unity and equality in Christ. His death on the cross and resurrection meant that both Jews and Gentiles would be extended the gift of salvation by grace through faith. It put hostility toward each other to death. That's good news!

Read verses 17-18 (page 896). How does it say everyone comes to God?

Thru Him (Jesus) we have access to God.

Through the same Holy Spirit. Unified in Christ. It doesn't seem possible — but God makes it possible when we put on the breastplate of righteousness.

We have a birdfeeder hanging in the tree outside our dining room and it provides us an ongoing study of nature. A dozen little house wrens will be happily gorging themselves on the tasty seeds when suddenly a blue jay alights on a nearby branch. The wrens fly off in a huff. With the wrens gone, more jays fly in to enjoy the seed — until a dove arrives. Away go the jays, leaving the dove to himself. The doves are peculiar. Not only do they refuse to eat with birds of a different species, they don't particularly desire to dine with their fellow doves. When a second dove arrives at the feeder, the two fuss at each other until one of them leaves or moves to the other side of the tree. Watching this daily battle of the birds makes me wonder if even wildlife can't get along, how can we humans ever manage? We can't without putting on the breastplate of righteousness. We need to keep it on through everything we do until we become a gleaming reflection of Jesus Christ.

Read the following verses and note what they say about unity in Christ.

Galatians 3:26-28 (Page 892)

all sons of God thru faith in Christ Jesus ... all one in Christ Jesus

Colossians 3:7-11 (Page 903)

live a life worthy of the Lord & please Him in g way. Bearing fruit, being strengthened c all power according to His glorious might. so that you may have great endurance & patience. Joyfully giving thx to Father

Philippians 2:1-3 (Page 900)

... make my joy complete by being likeminded ... - consider others better than yourself

The last phrase of Philippians 2:3 holds a secret to the path of unity in Christ: count others as more significant than yourselves. Think about the people in your life who are a source of irritation or pain — the ones who require extra grace. Maybe there is even someone for whom you feel hatred or bitterness. Take a moment and ask God to show you how He feels about them.

Write down your honest response about what the verse exhorts you to do.

God loves ALL of us as tho there was only 1 of us !!

What is being asked of us in these passages does not primarily benefit the people who came to your mind. It benefits you — sets you free from the power they hold over your life through your attitude toward them.

Read Proverbs 21:21, page 496.

When we put on the breastplate of righteousness and pursue unfailing love in our relationships, God offers tremendous blessings in return. Only His spirit within us enables us to behave in opposition to our natural human nature.

He who pursues, Righteousness & love finds life, prosperity + honor

Read Ephesians 2:19-22 (page 896) and note the various ways we are described in this passage.

OK MY!!

We are members of God's family — Jewish and Gentile believers — carefully joined together in Him. The Message puts it like this:

> God is building a home. He's using us all — irrespective of how we got here — in what he is building... He's using you, fitting you in brick by brick, stone by stone, with Christ Jesus as the cornerstone that holds all the parts together. We see it taking shape day after day — a holy temple built by God, all of us built into it, a temple in which God is quite at home.

As believers in God's family we become righteous the minute we accept Jesus Christ as our Savior because His blood provides a covering for our sin. However, that does not mean we never sin again, never behave badly, think wrongly, or choose poorly. Living righteously is a minute by minute choice, a process that takes shape day after day as we allow God's Holy Spirit to work through us.

In response to Steve's prayers, Jeff was reconciled to God the Father through His Son Jesus. He came to know "the one God and one Mediator who can reconcile God and humanity — the man Christ Jesus" (1 Timothy 2:5, page 910). As a result, Jeff was empowered to put on the breastplate of righteousness and live as a new creation in Christ.

Steve felt led to pray for all the guys on his floor. He longed to see them united in Christ. It is only our unity in Christ that makes it possible to break down the walls of separation with others. It takes God working through us to reflect His love and righteousness to those around us in the circumstances we face.

Closing Prayer

Lord, thank You for making me a new creation in Christ — a masterpiece in Your eyes designed to walk in righteousness. Help me to clothe myself with love, which will bind me together with others in perfect unity as we submit to the lordship of Jesus. Fill me with joy, grow me to maturity, and let me be an encouragement to others. Enable me to live in harmony and peace, knowing that you, the God of love and peace, are always with me (Ephesians 2:10, page 896; Colossians 3:14, page 904; 2 Corinthians 13:11, page 889).

Personal Reflection and Application

I see

I believe

I will

Thoughts, Notes, and Prayer Requests

chapter 3

BOLD FAITH

Kirsten Powers, now a popular national television news correspondent, loved her life. After six years in Washington D.C. as an appointee in a presidential administration, she found herself living in New York, still deeply involved in politics. Kirsten surrounded herself with left-leaning intellectuals, most of whom were atheists. She herself wavered between atheism and agnosticism. "I sometimes hear Christians talk about how terrible life must be for atheists," she writes, "but our lives were not terrible. Life actually seemed pretty wonderful, filled with opportunity and good conversation and privilege."

As a single woman, she told a friend her only deal-breaker in dating was someone religious. Then, several months into a relationship, her boyfriend asked her if she believed Jesus was her Savior. "My heart sank," she said. "I started to panic. Oh no, I thought, he's crazy." She answered him with an emphatic NO, adding that she'd never change her mind.

Then he asked the magic question for a liberal, "Do you think you could keep an open mind about it?" And thus began Kirsten's journey toward Christ.

Kirsten said she was both creeped out and intrigued by what her boyfriend told her about God. Those emotions continued as she went with him to church. There she realized that even if Christianity wasn't the real thing, neither was atheism. She first ventured into the Bible on her own, then began attending a group Bible study at the advice of a friend. A knot formed in her stomach the first time she went because she thought "only weirdos and zealots went to Bible studies."

Kirsten doesn't exactly recall what was said that day. "All I know is that when I left, everything had changed. I'll never forget standing outside that apartment on the Upper East Side and saying to myself, *It's true. It's completely true.* The world looked entirely different, like a veil had been lifted off. I had not an iota of doubt. I was filled with indescribable joy."[1]

Like Kirsten Powers, when the Apostle Paul encountered Jesus everything about his life changed. He was compelled after that to take up the shield of faith and share the Good News of Jesus with others. He paid a high price for this. Once, out of concern for the believers in Corinth who were being influenced by smooth-talking men who were critical of him, he listed all he'd endured as a result of his commitment to Christ.

Read 2 Corinthians 11:23-28 (page 888).

Whoa! That's some list of trouble, isn't it? Yet through all he endured, Paul exhibited a strength that flies in the face of human reasoning. He said, "By God's grace and mighty power, I have been given the privilege of serving him by spreading this Good News" (Ephesians 3:7, page 896). He counted it as a joy and honor to share Christ with others no matter what the cost.

Read 2 Corinthians 12:9-10 (page 888).
Why does Paul say he takes pleasure in his suffering?

... So that the power of Christ may dwell in me, ... Content I weakness, insult, hardship, persecution, & calamities for sake of Christ — ... for whenever I am weak, then I am strong.

Experience taught that the greater his needs, the greater he experienced God's power. His weakness formed a conduit for God to work through. As he leaned into his shield of faith, God showed up.

A closer look at the Roman shield shows us what a perfect analogy it offers for our faith. The shield consisted of as many as six layers of specially tanned animal hide woven tightly together to form an impenetrable barrier. Shaped like a door, its length and width completely covered the soldier. In fact, the Greek word *thureos* used to describe the shield of faith in Ephesians literally means door. Paul's shield of faith became a door to Jesus for others.

There is another reason Paul persevered in the midst of his suffering.

Read Ephesians 3:1 (page 896).

By whom did Paul consider himself to be imprisoned? Interesting, isn't it? A Roman guard shared Paul's space 24 hours a day, and the Roman government planned to put him on trial to decide his fate, yet Paul sees himself as a prisoner of Christ Jesus. In spite of his circumstances, Paul understood God's sovereignty. As fearsome and powerful as the Romans were, their ability to determine Paul's future was submitted to God's control. Paul knew his imprisonment would not last one second longer than God allowed. The Romans thought they could control his destiny. In reality, they might have bound him in chains, but God held the key to the lock.

Read the following verses and note common themes:

Job 42:2 (page 414)

I know you can do all things, and that no purpose of yours can be ~~thwarted~~ thwarted.

Philippians 4:13 (page 901)

I can do all things thru Him who strengthens me.

Isaiah 43:13 (page 550)

I am God, + also henceforth I am HE. there is no one who can deliver from my hand; I work + who can hinder it.

Paul held a strong faith that God's ultimate plan would unfold through his imprisonment. He knew a godly purpose existed behind his suffering. His confidence benefited other believers, strengthened their faith, and gave them courage in their own trials. His captivity also benefited the guards who held him — the Roman authorities with whom he shared Christ — as well as their families. Paul saw every day of his imprisonment as an opportunity to further the Gospel.

Are you caught in a painful struggle? Do you feel powerless in your circumstances? How can you apply the verses you've just read to your current situation?

God can & is working thru my Cardiac issues

In Ephesians 3, Paul drives home the point that the death and resurrection of Jesus Christ allows those who believe the Good News to share equally in God's riches because they are all His children (v. 6). God planned this from the beginning: for equality among His creation. That plan was carried out through Jesus (v. 11). It's a plan almost too remarkable to grasp — steeped in an inconceivable love and desire for relationship.

Read Ephesians 3:12 (page 896).
With what attitude can we enter into God's presence?

We have access to God in boldness & confidence thru faith in Him.

Focus on the magnitude of that phrase. God wants us to approach Him without hesitancy, without shame or guilt. We are fully welcome at all times because we are His family — His children. It's the way our five-year-old granddaughter, Milo, bounds into our house. She doesn't bother knocking, but flings open the door, knowing we'll drop everything and meet her with delight. That's how this verse says we can approach God. Imagine yourself for a minute flinging open the door to God's throne of grace. Imagine Him greeting you with delight.

What comes to mind as you think about this?

Lily !!

Read Ephesians 3:12 (page 901). Why is it we can come boldly and confidently into God's presence?

thru faith in Him

HE IS
ABLE

Christ made it all possible when He died on the cross. His shed blood became like a backstage pass allowing us bold and confident access to God, any time, any place. Whether or not we use the pass is up to us, dependent on our faith in Jesus Christ. Faith is the linchpin of our relationship with God. Hebrews 11:6 says it is impossible to please God without it.

What do the following verses say about faith?
Galatians 2:20 (page 891)

..."It is no longer I who live, but Christ who lives in me. And the life I live in the flesh, I now live by faith in the Son of God."

Hebrews 11:1-3 (page 926)

Faith is assurance of things hoped for, evidence of things not seen ... By faith ... what is seen was made from things unseen

Proverbs 3:5-6 (page 482)

Trust in the Lord i all your heart + lean not on your own understanding. In all your ways acknowledge Him + He will direct your path.

While faith first brings us to belief in Christ, it also matures our relationship with Him as we navigate life. Paul understood this and never went to battle without his shield of faith. A Roman soldier's shield would become stiff and unusable if not properly cared for because of its animal hide construction. Every morning, a soldier thoroughly oiled his shield to keep it soft and pliable. Failure to do so meant certain death on the battlefield.[2] Our faith works in the same way. It requires regular care to properly protect us.

The oil for the shield of faith is the Good News. Summarize the following verses.

Romans 1:17 (page 857)

The one who is Righteous will live by faith.

Romans 10:17 (page 864)

Faith comes thru hearing and hearing comes from Christ

The more we saturate our life with the oil of Good News, the more vibrant and life-changing our faith becomes. Our ability to live each day in the knowledge of our righteousness in Christ depends on how steeped we are in this truth. The more we access it, the easier it becomes to maintain boldness and confidence to approach God. Note key themes in the following verses:

Psalm 119:11 (page 468)

Thy word have I hid in my ♡, that I might not sin against thee —

Psalm 119:29 (page 469)

Remove from me falsehood + unfaithfulness + impart Your word to me

Psalm 119:61 (page 469)

The cords of wicked have enclosed + ensnared me, I have not forgotten Your law

Knowing God's Word and allowing it to influence our lives builds our faith in layers, protecting us as nothing else can. It literally transforms our minds and lives for good.

A Roman soldier did something else to increase his shield's effectiveness. Before going into battle, he placed it in a tub of water to completely saturate it. He knew the enemy would attack with flaming arrows and his wet shield would extinguish the arrows upon contact, rendering them ineffective.[3] It's easy to see why Paul used that analogy in Ephesians 6:16 instructing us to "hold up the shield of faith to stop the fiery arrows of the devil."

Satan targets our minds. He constantly shoots fiery arrows of doubt, hopelessness, envy, discontentment, and every other negative emotion with the capacity to threaten the life God designed for us.

Read John 10:10 (page 819).
What is our enemy's goal?

What is God's goal for us?

Now read John 14:21 (page 823). What does our obedience imply?

What is the result?

Love and revelation! We need to avoid the temptation to pick and choose areas of obedience if we want to know God's love more deeply. The more we meditate on God's ways, the easier it becomes to follow Him. Our trust grows as we engage in living and active conversation with God and through the Bible. The less we know what His Word says, the more difficult life becomes. Doubts crop, up paving the way for compromise, and soon everything breaks down. Incorporating a reliance upon God by understanding the truths of the Bible creates in us more peace and contentment for whatever we face, now and in the future.

The last verses of Ephesians 3 contain Paul's prayer for the people of Ephesus. It's a prayer for us as well. These beautiful words describe the incredible dimension of God's love.

Read Ephesians 3:14-20 (page 896) and describe the way our Creator loves us and how we are invited to respond:

"He will fill our inner being" His glorious strength,

Boundless! It's deeply moving to meditate on His goodness for us, isn't it? God's love for us, His power working in us, will accomplish infinitely more than we can even ask or think. God has no limits. His love for us surpasses all measurement. The more actively we maintain our shield of faith, the deeper our roots will grow into God's limitless love, keeping us strong and vibrant.

Closing Prayer

Father, teach me to walk by faith, not by sight because without faith it is impossible to please You. I know that You reward those who sincerely seek You. I understand that Your thoughts are nothing like mine, and Your ways are far beyond anything I can imagine. Give me grace to trust that You are with me and will protect me wherever I go. And may I always be ready to explain the hope I have in Christ with those who don't yet know Him (2 Corinthians 5:7 page 884; Hebrews 11:6 page 926; Isaiah 55:8-9, page 560; Genesis 28:58a, page 23; 1 Peter 3:15, page 936).

Personal Reflection and Application

I see

I believe

I will

Thoughts, Notes, and Prayer Requests

chapter 4

THE VALUE OF UNITY

C hurch split. Horrible words with horrible repercussions. The spiritual equivalent of divorce that tears church families asunder. It was the last thing I ever expected to happen to our church. It began with one disgruntled man talking persistently against the pastor. Almost overnight, a chasm opened up amongst us. On Sundays the aisle down the center of the sanctuary became an invisible barrier as we almost unconsciously divided ourselves up according to which side we were on — just like a wedding with the groom's side and the bride's side, only no one was celebrating.

Attendance dwindled as our focus turned away from worshipping God and settled on the differences we had with each other. People stopped speaking to each other. Lifelong friends no longer even made eye contact. No one was willing to concede anything, each believing they were "contending for the faith" (Jude v. 3, NIV).

The church building we'd built together and paid for through sacrificial offerings, donated talent, and countless hotdog and bake sales, fell into disrepair from lack of care literally and figuratively. Visitors stopped visiting, lives stopped being transformed, and some members became so embittered they left, never to darken the door of a church again. There were many things I didn't understand during this time, but I knew one thing for sure — this was not the way God's family should behave.

One truth we should never ignore when we become followers of Christ: Even after He has created us anew in Him, our old nature remains within reach. We can slip into old thought patterns and behaviors with shocking ease the minute we lay down any piece of the spiritual armor God provides us.

In Ephesians 4, Paul stresses the importance of maintaining unity within the body of Christ. He exhorts us to treat each other with gentleness and longsuffering, "bearing with one another in love" (v. 2,

NKJV). As we read in an earlier lesson, we are no longer to let various cultures or worldly opinions divide us. We are to "be kind to each other, tenderhearted, forgiving one another, just as God through Christ has forgiven [us]" (v. 32, page 897).

Read what the following verses have to say about the body of Christ:
Galatians 6:10 (page 894) ~ do good to all people
Romans 12:4-5 (page 866) each member belongs to all other
1 Corinthians 12:26 (page 877) If I don't suffer all suffer
1 Corinthians 3:9 (page 871) We are God's fellow workers ~
What picture do these verses paint for you of how God's family should operate?

It sounds wonderful, doesn't it? Like a perfect family we'd all like to be adopted into. Unity does not happen automatically just because we are followers of Christ. It takes solid determination to maintain it.

Read Ephesians 4:1-6 (page 897) and list the various instructions you see.
Live life worthy of the calling
Be humble, patient & gentle, bearing w one another & love
Keep unity of the Spirit

Did you notice the beginning instruction summarizes those that follow? Lead a life worthy of God's calling. How basic can it get? It's like Paul is saying, "You're an heir to God's kingdom, so live like it. Bear His name well."

Achieving unity also takes honesty. We are to "tell our neighbors the truth, for we are all parts of the same body" (Ephesians 4:25, page 897). When we put on the "belt of truth" described in God's armor in Ephesians 6, we help ensure harmony with our brothers and sisters in Christ.

Without a doubt, the belt performed the most vital service for the Roman soldier, serving multiple purposes. The belt provided a resting place for the shield, held the sword in a ready position, and kept the breastplate steady. The belt was crucial to all the other pieces of armor.[1] No wonder this is the very first piece of armor to which Paul refers. Jesus Himself is described as "the way, the truth, and the life" (John 14:6), and to be united in Him means to walk in truth.

We need to take an honest look at our relationships and see others the way God does rather than focusing on faults.

What does Ephesians 4:2 say should be the basis for making allowances for the faults of others?

Do you feel a sense of conviction when you think about this? Is it your natural inclination to make allowances for the faults of your fellow Christians, or do you lean more toward judging them? Paul encourages us to bear with the weaknesses of those sitting across the aisle from us. To avoid the kind of divisive impasse our church experienced, we need to be patient with each other. Sometimes love requires us to do exactly the opposite of what we want to do.

According to Ephesians 4:3-6, why are we to bind ourselves together with peace?

→ *United in spirit* ~

Could Paul make it any clearer? We are one in Christ. End of story. To make sure his point is taken, in those verses one is reiterated seven times! No room exists in the body of Christ for anything other than unity. When we take any action that moves us away from unity, either individually or as a group, we step onto very dangerous and destructive territory.

As a pastor once said, unity is not the same as uniformity. It does not mean we all must think and act identically. God created us to be unique individuals. Not even our own two thumbprints are the same, so neither should we expect our thoughts, perspectives, or approach to life to match others'. In fact, when our differences are placed in God's hands, the body of Christ becomes a force to be reckoned with!

Read Ephesians 4:7-13 (page 897).
What does verse 7 tell us about our individuality?

Read what the following verses say about the body of Christ and sum up the message of both passages.
1 Corinthians 12:12-22 (page 877)

Romans 12:3-10 (page 866)

Both of these passages make it clear God granted each one of us specific abilities to enhance His body of believers. As we function the way God created us to alongside others, we become a more effective witnesses of God's Word. Did you notice the emphasis on the equality of each gift, that each is equally needed for the body to function as intended? If we feel we are not a necessary part of the body of Christ, we are drawing an erroneous conclusion that not only hinders our own faith walk, but also hinders the effectiveness of the whole body. Every gift is equal in its necessity.

The Romans passage also stresses the importance of love in maintaining unity. We are to love with genuine affection and take delight in honoring each other (v. 9-10, page 866). A good way to develop your ability to love is to choose someone on the "other side of the aisle" and ask God to enable you to take delight in honoring them every time you see them, speak of them, or think of them. The idea might make you cringe right now, but this practice produces righteousness and glory for God.

Take a moment right now and think of one person in your commu
you are least interested in loving. When someone comes to mind, ask
God to show you how to move toward this person and treat them
with the real love that only He can cultivate in your heart.

Paul outlines a specific purpose for maintaining unity within God's
family and for developing the specific abilities God grants us.

Read Ephesians 4:14-16 (page 897) and list the results of unity.

When we speak the truth in love, we grow in every way more like
Christ. Verse 16 is a perfect summation: As each part does its own
special work, it helps the other parts grow, so that the whole body
is healthy and growing and full of love. Unity makes the individual
stronger and the entire body of Christ stronger. It's a rich and satisfying experience to be a part of something healthy, growing and full
of love. More importantly, living in unity creates a desire in observ-
ers to join in. This is a definition for evangelism — drawing people
into the circle of God's love.

The truth of God's love is a powerful weapon in the relational battles we face. As we digest God's Word and let it transform us more
into His likeness, we mature in our ability to love well.

What do the following verses tell us about the Word of God?
2 Timothy 3:16-17 (page 915)

Psalm 119:105 (page 470)

Proverbs 30:5 (page 503)

John 8:32 (page 817)

These passages give many good reasons for buckling on the belt of Truth. It provides protection for our entire being, physically, mentally, emotionally, and spiritually. When we neglect to fortify ourselves with the life-truths of God's Word, our thought process, perspective, and way we view life immediately begin to deteriorate. We start to feel condemned by God rather than accepted by Him. Our behavior deteriorates as we become more controlled by our fleshly, worldly nature than by our new spiritual nature, making unity possible.

Read Ephesians 4:17-19 (page 897).

Have you ever felt hopeless confusion? Clarity can be found within God's Word. Just open your Bible and start reading — it doesn't matter where — and your confusion will start to dissipate in the light of God's Truth. The Holy Spirit within you will make the Word of God applicable to your circumstances. God's Word will keep you from wandering away into darkness as it keeps your mind open to His teaching and guidance.

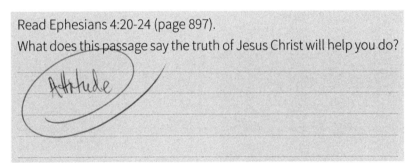

Read Ephesians 4:20-24 (page 897).
What does this passage say the truth of Jesus Christ will help you do?

Attitude

After we are reconciled to God through the blood of Jesus Christ, He continues to work in us to help us lay aside our old self and grow in righteousness and truth. Jesus Christ becomes an ongoing, intentional way of life.

What does Romans 12:2 (page 866) say about this?

The level of transformation you experience is in direct correlation to how consistently you put on the belt of Truth by reading God's Word. The Message paraphrase puts it like this:

> Don't become so well-adjusted to your culture that you fit into it without even thinking. Instead, fix your attention on God. You'll be changed from the inside out. Readily recognize what he wants from you, and quickly respond to it. Unlike the culture around you, always dragging you down to its level of immaturity, God brings the best out of you, develops well-formed maturity in you.

What God produces in you is best. He helps you grow into satisfying, well-formed maturity! It can only happen by consistently wearing the belt of Truth.

Paul writes a simple list of dos and don'ts. As you read Ephesians 4:25-32 (page 897), place each instruction under the appropriate column.

Do	Don't

As you look over your two lists, underline your strengths and weaknesses.

What can you do to transform some of your weaknesses into strengths?

"If I agreed ī you, we'd both be wrong."

Here's something to add to the don't list. Don't let yourself become discouraged. Transformation is an ongoing process. God never stops His loving work within us.

Read Philippians 2:12-13 (page 900).

One Sunday morning when our church reached its lowest point, a young man who was as faded and worn as his blue jeans stumbled into the sanctuary after the service had begun. He slipped into a back pew looking uncomfortable and out-of-place. When the service concluded, our pastor hurried to meet him before he could quietly escape. The man's name was Mike and he explained he was an alcoholic, three days sober and desperate to stay that way. Our church seemed his last resort. What none of us realized that Sunday was that Mike would turn out to be as important to us as we were to him.

That very week, Mike began his relationship with Jesus Christ and our broken church family made it our mission to help him rebuild his life. He blossomed under our care through God's redeeming love. He devoured the Bible, never missed a church event, and grew stronger every day. Soon his parents were attending church with him, curious to see the reason behind the dramatic change in their son.

Then one Sunday, several months after his first visit, Mike didn't show up at church. I immediately knew something was wrong. As worship began and Mike still wasn't there, I grew so concerned I finally whispered to my husband I was going to check on him. I found him at his camp trailer home, eyes bleary, too ashamed to look at me. I strained to understand his mumbled explanation of how he'd agreed to meet a friend at the bar the night before, wanting to tell him about his new-found life. Just like that, his months of hard-fought sobriety came to an end. Heartsick, I assured him of God's love and our commitment to him. He shook his head, awash with shame and hopelessness.

Just then there was a knock on the door. Another church member, also concerned, had slipped out of church to check on Mike. Every few minutes, another knock on the door announced yet another worried church member who didn't know the others were already there. The last to arrive was our pastor, who was also worried about Mike and wondered why his church members kept leaving. He had hurriedly finished the service and headed for Mike's trailer. There we all gathered, from both sides of the aisle, bunched shoulder to shoulder in the tiny camp trailer as we surrounded Mike and prayed in a spirit of unity.

All those months ago, when Mike stumbled into our church searching for redemption, none of us realized he brought with him an avenue for our own redemption. God continually pursues His children with love and truth. He identifies us as His own (verse 30). His love knows no measure, and He does infinitely more than we can ever ask or think (Ephesians 3:20, page 896).

In the same way God did not give up on Mike, He also did not give up on our congregation, pursuing us toward unity in Him. He's not giving up on you and your community either.

Closing Prayer

Lord, thank You for redeeming me through the blood of Jesus. Give me grace to be patient with others and to make allowance for each other's faults because of Your love. Thank You for the truth of who I am in Christ and for giving me eyes to see others as You do. May I speak the truth in love in all circumstances, growing in every way more like Christ. And may I daily put on the new nature, created to be like You — righteous, holy, tenderhearted, and forgiving (Ephesians 4:2, 15, 24, 32, page 896-897).

Personal Reflection and Application

I see

I believe

I will

Thoughts, Notes, and Prayer Requests

chapter 5

LIVING IN THE LIGHT

D riving toward the house where our mother grew up, my brother took advantage of a two-mile shortcut through a narrow, winding gorge over the objections of his wife. The sharp S-corners created anxiety in her about cars coming in the opposite direction. To make the situation even more edgy, it was dark. Jim assured her any oncoming vehicles would be announced well in advance by their headlights. "But what if they're driving with their lights off?" she asked.

"Judi! What kind of fool would drive through the gorge at night without any lights?" he answered.

The very next weekend, Judi travelled with my mom through the very same gorge late at night. Halfway through, both headlights on my mom's car suddenly dimmed and then failed completely. No pullouts or even shoulder space was available to stop safely. Mom had no option but to continue through, slowing to a crawl as she navigated the sharp curves through the inky night. By the time they reached the ranch, mom and Judi, though safe and thankful, were completely shaken. Judi marched straight up to my brother and demanded, "So Jim! You want to know what kind of fool drives through the gorge at night without their headlights?"

The darker it gets, the more we rely on light. It has a great way of clearing things up. The English language offers many idioms involving light such as, "shed a little light on the subject" or "suddenly the light dawned." The Bible speaks often about light and darkness. In fact, Jesus referred to Himself as light. "I am the light of the world," He said. "If you follow me, you won't have to walk in darkness, because you will have the light that leads to life" (John 8:12, page 817).

In Ephesians 5, Paul encourages us to "live as people of light" (v. 8), with light representing our new nature in Jesus Christ.

Read Ephesians 5:1-2 (page 897).
Who are we to imitate?

No small task, huh? Imitate God in everything you do. This daunting command may seem impossible, but in truth it becomes easier as we walk closer with Jesus — the source of light. With His guidance, it becomes easier to navigate those narrow, dangerous S-curves of life.

This brings us to the next piece of God's armor: the sword of the Spirit which is His Word (Ephesians 6:17, page 898). As we wield the sword of the Spirit, God's Truth cuts through the lies that try to blind us on the road of life. It's the only offensive piece in the armor, which Psalm 119:105 describes as a guide to our feet and a light for our path.

The Roman soldier had five swords at his disposal, each of varying length to serve different purposes. The deadliest of the five was approximately 19 inches long, and both sides of this blade were sharpened to a razor's edge.[1] The sword of the Spirit is a brutal weapon against the darkness around us. When the enemy comes in to attack our relationships, it's the sword of God's Word that exposes our innermost thoughts and desires, cutting between soul and spirit, between joint and marrow, exposing us to the One to whom we are accountable so He can heal and reconcile (Hebrews 4:12, page 922).

Throughout the entire book of Ephesians, Paul keeps bringing us back to love. It is the key to everything. What we find, though, is that it is difficult to continually love well. This is why we need Christ, not only to set an example, but to empower us with the ability to love rightly. We love each other because He loved us first (1 John 4:19, page 943). We follow Christ by behaving in love. God's transforming love within us empowers us to do so. The more we experience His love, the more adept we become at following the light God shines on our path.

Read Ephesians 5:3-9 (page 897).

Did you notice Paul's reference to light and darkness? Darkness refers to our nature when we were dead to disobedience and enslaved to sin (Ephesians 2:1). We were unable to avoid sin. But now we are different. We are new creatures in Christ Jesus empowered to love well because God has shown His light in our hearts so we can know His glory seen in the face of Jesus Christ (2 Corinthians 4:6, page 884). We are light in the Lord (Ephesians 5:8 NASB). We have a new identity in Christ and His light is part of our being. The fruit of light is goodness, righteousness, and truth.

Given our new nature, we desire to do what is good, right, and true. Still, the old nature often tries to take over the spirit of God in us, and old habits and thought patterns start creeping in again — causing us to make poor choices.

What are the poor choices listed in this passage?

_____

_____

_____

_____

John Piper sheds light on our true identity in Christ as a "new creation":

> What happens in the new creation or the new birth? What
> God creates in the new birth is not a sinless Christian. What
> he creates is an embattled, not-yet-perfect, Spirit-empow-
> ered, persevering, Christ-treasuring, sin-hating, new being
> — a new creation in Christ... [We have] new DNA and can-
> not be content with ongoing sinning in this life.[2]

Thus, Christians often find themselves in a difficult place when they
pick and choose the little bits of dark indulgences to entertain. In
reality, these "little" choices succeed in complicating things in a big
way over time, making the battle even more fierce. Famous preacher
Billy Sunday put it like this: "One reason sin flourishes is it is treated
like a cream puff rather than a rattle snake."[3]

Choosing to put on God's armor here and there keeps us in a state of
constant vulnerability. Holding up the shield of faith only now and
then makes it unwieldy and hard to handle. Leaving the sword of
the Spirit at our side makes us easy prey. The more fully we choose
to walk in the light, the more natural Christ-like behavior becomes.
Darkness complicates; light simplifies. Always. No exceptions.

What does Ephesians 5:4 tell us to replace sinful behavior with?

Does the power of thankfulness surprise you? How do you see gratitude as a way of avoiding poor choices?

Thankfulness to God is a key weapon against our old way of thinking and behaving because it helps us focus on the Source of light. It keeps our gaze locked on God rather than the darkness of our circumstances.

As we behold God's ways and His Word, we discover the keys to overcoming life's battles. For example, have you ever been reading your Bible and suddenly came across a verse or passage that exactly offers what you needed right at that moment? So precisely on target, you sat in awe, knowing God revealed to you those words at that precise time. The sword of the Spirit sliced out the very words you needed. This happened because you were reading His Word! Being in the Word enables you to apply the Scripture appropriately to your particular circumstances.

The sword of the Spirit isn't limited to when you're reading the Bible. The Holy Spirit will bring Bible verses to your mind when you pray, talk with other believers, and pay attention to ways He speaks to you. A thankful attitude keeps the blade of the sword sharp and ready, slicing through doubt and disappointment to reveal God's guidance. The sword of the Spirit is a weapon of discernment. It's of immeasurable value to a Christian when the enemy tries to confuse us.

Ephesians 5:6-7 warns about this.

What are the two don'ts it mentions?

_____

_____

_____

_____

Don't be fooled! Don't participate! The warning couldn't be more empathic. Without the protection of the armor of God, we succumb to lies and take the bait which lures us into participation. We hear these lures: What's the big deal? Who will know? I deserve it. Thousands of excuses rationalize our choice to give in to old, unhealthy living. With every unwise choice a new complication arises, making the path darker. Obedience to God begins to feel constricting and laborious — the exact opposite of how obedience should feel.

Read Matthew 11:28-30 (page 742).

Walking in obedience gives us rest for our soul. Choices that fail to align with God's will burden us — an inescapable fact we know to be true from our own experience.

What does Ephesians 5:9 (page 897) say?

_____

_____

_____

_____

Right and true! How could we ever want to go back to darkness once we've experienced light? God has made the choice so simple for us.

Ephesians 5:10 (page 897) is key to the whole chapter. What does it say?

How can we determine what pleases the Lord?

The belt of truth and sword of the Spirit never lead us astray. God's Word is truth; it is light. Choosing the light never needs rationalization. The minute we start to rationalize an action or decision, we must take a step back and carefully determine what pleases the Lord.

Read Ephesians 5:15-20 (page 897-898).

Don't be foolish! We are to make the most of every opportunity to understand God's ways and live them out. We are encouraged to cultivate a worshipful and thankful heart, being filled with the Spirit. This is how we live by the light of God's truth — a choice He blesses.

Read the following verses:
Psalm 119:30 (page 469)
John 14:15 (page 823)
Psalm 119:133 (page 471)

You will not, cannot go wrong when you set your mind to follow God. The more you live by His Word, the more light floods into your life. When challenges arise, you will have help making the right choices because God's word is influencing you; the sword of the Spirit is directing you. God wants you to live with an overall attitude of joy that is sourced in Him and not influenced by your circumstances. His joy is capable of transcending whatever you are experiencing and thankfulness is the conduit to the joy.

Read Ephesians 5:19-20 (page 898) and note what it tells us to do.

Something about the action of singing changes the attitude of the heart regardless of the situation. Singing praises sets up a barrier against darkness and reduces challenges to bearable proportions because we're focused on the Source of light and hope.

Did you notice the reference to thankfulness? What does Paul tell us to be thankful for (verse 20)?

It doesn't seem reasonable, does it? It's absolutely impossible logic! But we don't rely on limited human logic or ability to figure things out. We reject our old ways of thinking and determine to walk in the light. We do this through an ongoing attitude of thankfulness to God who holds all things in His hands and who has the power to accomplishing infinitely more than we might ask or think (Ephesians 3:20, page 896).

He is our light. He is our hope. He is our sword!

The final portion of Ephesians 5 into the next chapter addresses relationships. As we walk in the light, it affects all those who interact with us on a daily basis. Up to this point, Paul has taught about our relationship with God, with the world around us, and with fellow Christians. Now he brings our attention to marriage and family relationships.

Read Ephesians 5:21 (page 898). What is the instruction in this passage?

_____

_____

_____

_____

Healthy relationships flourish when each person sacrificially defers to the good of the other. God set the example when He gave up His Son. Jesus set the example when He gave up His life. Twice now in this chapter, Paul urges us to imitate God, to follow Jesus' example of selfless love. The concept of submission is found throughout the Bible — always with the same result. In giving up our self, we gain something of exquisitely greater value.

What are your thoughts about this?

It helps to remember who we are in Christ — His beloved sons and daughters. When we know who we are and whose we are, it becomes easier to trust God to work in our marriage and family relationships as we humbly submit. Paul saw himself in submission to God, not to the Roman soldiers who chained him. That perspective removed the bitterness, anger, resentment, and other negative emotions that could have naturally resulted from his unjust circumstances. His choice to submit to God enabled him to experience joy inwardly and spread light outwardly. That's how an attitude of submission works as God defines it.

Read Ephesians 5:22-30 (page 898). Jot down the phrases that compare the marriage relationship to the relationship Jesus Christ has with His church, His body of believers.

Again and again Paul shows us the analogy of the marriage relationship and the relationship of Christ and the church. Do you see how significant this is? God designed the marriage relationship as a tangible picture to the world of Christ's love for us! That picture becomes an accurate reflection of His love as a husband and wife selflessly express oneness with each other and oneness with Christ. Submission and respect are equal and necessary means of expressing and experiencing love on God's terms.

Closing Prayer

Father, thank You for offering Your Son as a sacrifice so that I could come into Your eternal family. May I walk in the light as You are in the light, taking no part in worthless deeds of darkness. Fill me anew with Your Spirit today and put a song of praise and thanksgiving in my heart. Teach me to love the way Christ does, in humility and submission, so that the world may know that I am Your disciple (Ephesians 5:1-2, 8, 19-20, 22-25, page 897-898; 1 John 1:7, NKJV; John 13:35, page 823).

Personal Reflection and Application

I see

I believe

I will

Thoughts, Notes, and Prayer Requests

FINDING PEACE ON HOLY GROUND

It was election night many years ago. My husband and I were glued to our television as the next president of the United States was in the process of being determined. I fidgeted with a mixture of anticipation and dread. It felt like such a crucial election with Christians on both sides of the equation praying fervently for their candidate. About half the results were in when my cousin, Neree, called me. "Get your Bible," she said. "Read Joshua 5:13-15 (page 170)."

The passage describes Joshua staring out over the city of Jericho that he was preparing to go to battle against. God had told Joshua his army would be victorious, but viewing the full scope of the enemy he faced still must have been somewhat daunting. Jericho had an impenetrable wall surrounding it and an army of fierce warriors protecting it.

Suddenly, Joshua saw a man standing in front of him with a drawn sword in his hand. Startled, Joshua demanded to know whose side he was on. The man's answer was simple: "Neither. As commander of the Lord's army I have now come."

Interesting! As commander of the Lord's army wouldn't you have expected him to say he was on the side of the Israelites? And yet he said neither side. He was simply from God. Of course we know that as God's chosen people, God was indeed on their side. The Old Testament is replete with stories of God fighting for the Israelites. But sometimes there is much more important at stake than which side we're on or who is right or wrong. What God wants from us is an undistracted focus on Him who holds all "sides" in His hands. Keep this story in mind as we work through this lesson. We will see how God-inspired peace is possible regardless of differences.

We all have strongly held beliefs and opinions. And we tend to feel ours are more logical than those of the opposing political party, or those of our spouse or neighbor. Differing opinions lead to divisions, and divisions often lead to trouble. But God's love is a powerful weapon against the divisions that can destroy our country, our marriages, our families. Rather than focusing on who's right or wrong, we need to focus on how we can accurately reflect the love of God even in our differences.

Putting on the whole armor of God and keeping it on is essential to Christ-followers because we are in a battle. We face political, societal and economical foes that are fierce, far beyond our ability to fight on our own, especially if we are not wearing protective armor. They are controlled by forces of darkness not even visible to us. In 2 Corinthians 2:10-11 (page 883) Paul urges us not to let Satan get a foothold in our relationships. We need to be aware of the forces of darkness around us.

Read the following verses and note what they say about our enemy:
John 10:10 (page 818)

_____

_____

_____

1 Peter 5:8 (page 937)

_____

_____

_____

_____

Ever on the prowl, the enemy is pure, relentless evil — and we are in his sights. He intends no glancing blows, no slight wounds. His aim is total destruction and being forewarned is being forearmed. It is to our far greater advantage to know our advocate, Jesus Christ, remembering that He is far above every ruler or authority or power of darkness (Ephesians 1:21, page 895) and that He forever lives to intercede on our behalf (Hebrews 7:25, page 923-924).

Note what the following verses say about Him:
1 John 2:1 (page 941)

1 John 4:4 (page 943)

Romans 8:34 (page 863)

God prevails now and forever! Jesus never stops advocating for us, even when we fail to follow God's precepts. He pursues us with a relentless love, seeking to remove everything that hinders our relationship with Him.

When you contemplate the reality of Jesus actually speaking to the Father on your behalf, what comes to mind?

It's amazing, isn't it? Jesus wasn't done loving us on the cross. He wasn't finished when He rose from the grave. He continues to love on our behalf each day. The Message paraphrases it like this:

> Who would dare tangle with God by messing with one of God's chosen? Who would dare even to point a finger? The One who died for us — who was raised to life for us! — is in the presence of God at this very moment sticking up for us. Do you think anyone is going to be able to drive a wedge between us and Christ's love for us? (Romans 8:35-37, page 863)

Nothing can separate us from God's love. Jesus is our ongoing advocate. Although our enemy is relentless, he will never be God's match. We can stand our ground and refuse to be daunted when the enemy tries to attack.

Read Ephesians 6:1-3 (page 898).

Obedience is central to our relationship with God. The earlier we learn the value of godly submission, the better it is for us. The more peace we will have in our homes and in our outside relationships.

The first place we begin to learn this is as children in regard to our parents. It is such a key concept that God included it in the 10 Commandments.

Read Exodus 20:12 (page 59).
What is the reward for honoring fathers and mothers?

_____

_____

_____

_____

Paul repeats this important command in Ephesians 6, reminding us that it is a command that comes with a promise. Honor your parents and "things will go well." If you are a parent, the connection between obedience and things going well presents itself daily. When our children obey us, life goes smoothly. The family thrives. When our children do not obey, when they balk at every instruction and employ creative ways to shirk expectations, home becomes a battlefield where no one thrives. Obedience is essential to thriving. As parents obey God, they cultivate good soil for their children to obey as well. They come to understand that our heavenly Father enhances their lives rather than restricting them. This leads perfectly into the next passage.

Read Ephesians 6:4 (page 898).

This tiny verse offers incalculable wisdom. Do not provoke your children to anger by the way you treat them. If you think about the commandments God provided us, He designed each to enhance our lives. He had our best interests in mind when He gave them. According to the last part of verse four, where does the discipline and instruction we are to raise our children with come from?

God! He provides perfect love and wisdom. The Creator of both parents and children knows everything from beginning to end. As we press into a close relationship with Him, He shows us how to discipline and instruct our children according to the personality and bent of each child. It's good to know we are not alone in the daunting task of raising our children. God is a constant source of wisdom and inspiration.

The challenges in family relationships, indeed all relationships, make the final piece of God's armor — the shoes of the gospel of peace — of utmost necessity. Paul writes, "For shoes, put on the peace that comes from the Good News so that you will be fully prepared" (Ephesians 6:15, page 923).

The shoes of the Roman soldier provided both offensive and defensive use. There were two parts to this piece of armor: the greave and the actual shoe. A piece of molded bronze or brass especially fitted to the soldier's leg and extending from the top of his knee to the upper portion of his foot created the greave. The shoe consisted of two pieces of metal to cover the top and bottom of the foot. Pieces of strong leather held the pieces together. The plating protected the soldier, while fearsome and dangerous one- to three-inch spikes attached to the bottom of the shoe provided the soldier with more offensive weapons.[1] Can you imagine being stomped by a soldier with bronze shoes equipped with three-inch spikes? You would be defenseless against such a weapon. Yet Paul chooses this fearsome piece of armor to illustrate the importance of peace!

What are your thoughts on this piece of God's armor?

Peace wielded correctly is actually an awesome weapon. Like the Roman soldiers' shoes, it is both offensive and defensive in nature. It not only protects us, but keeps our spiritual enemy at bay. This is especially important to remember as we look at a difficult passage in Ephesians regarding slavery. Today our culture sees slavery for what it is: abhorrent and illegal. Nevertheless, this passage provides us with instruction about the attitude we can have in Christ, even in grossly unfair circumstances.

Read Ephesians 6:5-9 (page 898).
As "slaves of Christ," what are we to do?

When Paul wrote Ephesians, more than six million people were enslaved in the Roman Empire.[2] Slavery was an accepted practice, though the treatment of slaves was often brutal and inhumane. Knowing this, Paul's instruction to slaves may shock you.

Looking deeper, we see an important qualifier mentioned twice.
What is it?

Slaves were to serve their masters as they would serve Christ. They were to work with enthusiasm as though they were working for the Lord. If God could enable slaves to have this attitude, how much more should we be able to make seemingly unbearable relationships bearable? Being reconciled with God through Jesus Christ makes intolerable injustice endurable. God's peace is like three-inch spikes enabling us to dig deep into His truth and love, making it impossible to slip down into bitterness and despair.

Remember how Paul viewed his imprisonment? He did not see himself as a prisoner of the Romans, but of God. When we face each circumstance with our eyes fixed on God, when we put every action and thought through the lens of His perspective, God becomes the only power controlling us. His love and peace trumps the evil that touches us. He protects our minds from bitterness, anger, and desire for revenge — emotions that can cause greater internal damage to us than the outward actions of others.

An ongoing attitude of supernatural, God-provided peace keeps us fully prepared for whatever life brings. The Greek word translated peace in Ephesians 6:15 conveys the concept of prevailing peace or conquering peace, implying a God-given ability to move forward in confident faith regardless of what we're facing.[3]

The Roman soldier kept his shoes bound tightly to his feet to prevent slippage, his feet stabilized regardless of the terrain. Similarly, we need to keep our minds tightly bound with the peace of God. His foundation offers security. He will keep in perfect peace all who trust in Him and fix their thoughts on Him (Isaiah 26:3, page 535).

The kind of peace Paul refers to is more than the peace that comes when we begin a relationship with Christ. The "peace that comes from the Good News so that you will be fully prepared" protects us in the ongoing battle with sin and helps us to overcome daily. Even Christ-followers can allow all kinds of destructive thoughts and choices to inhibit our quality of life. But God intends for us to experience something greater. He offers us prevailing peace.

Read the following verses and note what they say about peace.
Colossians 3:15 (page 904)

Philippians 4:7 (page 901)

Psalm 119:165 (page 471)

Did you notice the powerful words used to describe true peace? It rules, it guards, it keeps us from stumbling. It exceeds our understanding. How fantastic! When we bind our feet with the peace of God, nothing can defeat us. As it says in Romans 8, if God is for us, who can ever be against us? Nothing can separate us from His love.

> Neither death nor life, neither angels nor demons, neither our fears for today nor our worries about tomorrow — not even the powers of hell can separate us from God's love. No power in the sky above or in the earth below — indeed, nothing in all creation will ever be able to separate us from the love of God that is revealed in Christ Jesus our Lord.

> –Romans 8:38-39, page 863

Oh, how well-protected we are when we put on the whole armor of God. We are undefeatable in every way imaginable. When Joshua faced the Commander of the Lord's army, he fell face-down on the ground in reverence and asked, "What message does my Lord have for his servant?"

The Commander replied, "Take off your sandals, for the place where you are standing is holy" (Joshua 5:13-15, page 170,171). Right there overlooking enemy territory, Joshua was on holy ground because the presence of God was there! Never forget that when you are aligned with God the ground around you is holy. It does not belong to the enemy. Whatever battle you face today, whatever attack of the enemy threatens your physical, emotional, or spiritual well-being, you do not have to fear. When you align with God, He enables you to stay in perfect peace and walk in relational harmony. So strap on every piece of armor as tightly as you can and march forward in confidence, knowing that you are a vital part of God's army.

Closing Prayer

Father, I am so grateful You are not a God of disorder but of peace. Help my family honor the first commandment that it may go well for us. Show us how to serve those in authority with sincerity of heart, working with enthusiasm as unto You. Help me this day to be strong in You and in Your mighty power that I may stand firm against the strategies of the devil. Thank You for the wonderful knowledge that I can do everything through Christ who strengthens me. I Now I release my burdens to You, knowing that You will protect and care for me and my loved ones (1 Corinthians 14:33, page 879; Ephesians 6:2, 5-7, 10-11, page 898; Philippians 4:13, page 901).

Personal Reflection and Application

I see

I believe

I will

Thoughts, Notes, and Prayer Requests

chapter 7

THE WEAPON
OF PRAYER

A t war with the King of Israel, the King of Aram was at his wit's end. Every time he planned an attack, someone leaked word of the exact time and location he planned to strike. "Which of you is the traitor?" he demanded of his men. "Who has been informing the King of Israel of my plans?"

"It's not us," his officers insisted. "That prophet Elisha from Israel tells his king what you say even in the privacy of your bedroom!"

"Then find where he is so I can send troops to seize him."

The officers immediately began their search for Elisha. They found him in the city of Dothan and hurriedly sent word to their king. A great army of chariots and horses gathered and raced to surround the city. Unaware of the impending danger, Elisha's servant got up early the next morning and went outside. Terror turned his knees to jelly as he saw enemy troops, horses, and chariots everywhere he looked. He fled back inside. "Oh sir!" he cried to Elisha. "We are surrounded by the enemy. There are troops and horses and chariots everywhere! What are we going to do?"

Elisha didn't blink an eye. He looked at his terrified servant and spoke calmly. "Don't be afraid. There are far more on our side than on theirs!" Then Elisha prayed a simple prayer: "Oh Lord, open his eyes and let him see!" No begging, no pleading, no desperate bargaining. Just a handful of words to his sovereign God who held all power and consequence in His hands.

God heard the prayer and opened the young man's eyes to the invisible reality of their circumstances: the hillsides around them teemed with God's troops, God's horses, and chariots of fire! Their enemy may have surrounded them but God surrounded their enemy (2 Kings 6:8-17, page 287).

Roman soldiers wore seven pieces of armor: a helmet, breastplate, shield, belt, sword, shoes, and lance. Interestingly, Paul only draws a spiritual analogy to six pieces. He does not mention the lance. However, in the final verse summing up the importance of putting on the whole armor of God, Paul urges us to do one final thing which has the power to accomplish spiritually what a lance could accomplish physically. He tells us to pray at all times and on every occasion (Ephesians 6:18, page 898).

The lances used in ancient days came in a variety of lengths and sizes. The ones used by the Macedonians were 21 to 24 feet long — the length of a telephone pole. Imagine the strength required to throw such a lance! Other lances were very short, used for striking an enemy within close proximity. Most soldiers kept a variety of lances at hand. Similarly, we can send up prayers for every circumstance. Sometimes a short prayer like, "Help God!" is all it takes. Other times we need to contend in prayer over time until we feel released or see the breakthrough.

The typical Roman lance was about six feet long, designed to be thrown from afar. This allowed the soldiers to strike the enemy before they could penetrate their encampment. The lance had an iron head at the top and an iron shaft at the bottom, each about three feet in length. In other words, all six feet of the Roman lance was made of solid iron. If a soldier wanted to make his lance even more deadly, he loaded the head with extra iron. The heavier the lance head, the further it flew and the deadlier the strike.[1]

It's not difficult to draw an analogy between the lance and prayer. Prayer strikes with powerful force and prevents the enemy from penetrating our minds. Prayer is never out of reach and provides us with power and protection. There is no limit to how far our prayers can reach and how deep they can penetrate.

Simply put, prayer is communication with God. On page after page in the Bible, men and women, kings and communities talked with God. Prayer offers us a power line connecting us to the One who created heaven and earth. Many different Greek and Hebrew words in the original scriptures translate into the word prayer in the English language, and each conveys a different type or level of communication with God.

In the New Testament, the most common word for prayer comes from the Greek word *proseuche*. It shows up more than 120 times, including twice in Ephesians 6:18 which sums up the passage on spiritual armor. This word depicts something much more than just simple prayer. It conveys the idea of coming face-to-face with God, surrendering your life to Him and consecrating it on an ongoing basis. This word also conveys the idea of thanking God in advance for what He's going to do in your life.[2] You can see then how prayer, sharpened with thanksgiving, is like a lance in our hands — offering a long reach of protection from the enemy's attacks.

Read Ephesians 6:18 (page 898) and note everything it says about prayer.

Prayer works at all times, every occasion! It should be like breathing for us — instinctive and life-sustaining. But in reality prayer is often like breathing while swimming — we need intentional thought and experience for it to become instinctive.

> Read what the following verses have to say about this.
> Romans 12:12 (page 866)
> 1 Thessalonians 5:16-18 (page 907)
> Philippians 4:6 (page 901)
> Colossians 4:2 (page 904)
> Each verse encourages us to pray. Did you notice anything else these verses tell us to do?
>
> *Rejoice, prayer & ceasing, give thx*
> *con tinue in prayer*
> *Be mindful*
> *keep alert*
> *Be thankful*

Be thankful! To utilize prayer as the weapon it's intended to be, we must weight it with thankfulness. An attitude of thanksgiving keeps our circumstances and relationships in proper perspective. Regardless of how hopeless a situation appears from our human vantage point, thankfulness raises our perspective to God's viewpoint, from which nothing is impossible!

> Read the following verses.
> Luke 1:37 (page 780) — *Nothing is impossible c God —*
> Mark 9:23 (page 769) — *Anything is possible —*
> Matthew 19:26 (page 750) *c God anything is possible*

Nothing is impossible for God. Nothing limits Him — not anything or anyone. Our prayers access His power and presence to save, heal, deliver, reconcile, restore, provide, guide, and protect.

Now go back to Ephesians 6:18 (page 989). How does it tell us to pray?

To pray in the Spirit is to transcend the limitations of the physical realm and move into the spiritual realm.[3] It moves us beyond our limited perspective and capability and gives us access to God's limitless capability.

What circumstance in your life looks hopeless to you right now?

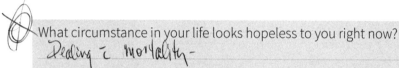

Dealing c mortality –

Try this: Take a moment and write out a prayer about this situation. Start by thanking God for how He is at work and what He will accomplish. Focus your prayer on applying God's unlimited power and love toward all those involved. Finish your prayer with strong statements of trust in God's omniscience, believing that He knows best how to resolve the situation.

There's nothing wrong with prayers of request or pleading for intervention. God loves it when we come to Him and is always listening.

Read the following verses:
1 Timothy 2:1-3 (page 910)
Luke 18:7 (page 800)

God hears and responds to all our prayers. His answers are not always what we expect, and His timing is sometimes different than what we hoped for, but He never ignores us. He is never sleeping or un-available. We can count on God's love, goodness, and faithfulness to us. When we are tempted to become discouraged or disheartened in prayer, it helps to refocus on the beauty and majesty of God. ("Our Father who art in heaven, hallowed be Thy name.") Pray with a heart that acknowledges our need for Jesus. ("Your kingdom come, your will be done on earth as it is in heaven.") Pray in faith, confident that all God's promises are "yes" in Christ Jesus (2 Corinthians 1:20) — such as our daily bread, forgiveness, and deliverance from evil. As we pray in agreement with God's heart for our circumstances, we often find that the Holy Spirit gives us a calm confidence in what our loving, all-powerful God will accomplish, even if the results are not exactly how we imagined. Prayer helps keep our faith strong and growing as we center our prayers around the power of God and maintain an attitude of thankfulness. It enables His spirit to calm us and opens our eyes to the invisible reality of our situation.

Elisha's story is a perfect example of this. He did not fall to his knees pleading for God's intervention in this desperate situation. He did not point out to God that there were only two of them against an entire army. God knew that already. Elisha simply prayed for the ability to see from God's perspective. And from that perspective the truth became visible — the truth that still applies to us today: God's army is always bigger, it's always stronger, and it always surrounds His children even if his deliverance is spiritual, not physical. We are never left defenseless or alone.

Read the following verses:
Psalm 145:18-19 (page 479)
Hebrews 4:16 (page 922)

There is immense comfort when we pray, isn't there, a greater aware-ness of God's nearness. This underscores the importance of prayer — active communication with God. As we grow in prayer, sometimes we benefit by setting aside our prayer lists for a time. There's noth-ing wrong with sincerely praying through a list of requests, but this can easily turn into one-way conversation with us talking and God listening. Without a list to narrow the parameters of our prayers, we can open up an avenue to listen and commune with God with an open heart. In this way, God reassures us He knows what's best and will guide us through our circumstances.

This open, two-way communion with God enables us to relinquish our idea of what the answer to prayer should look like and trust God's answer — whatever shape it comes in. It keeps us confident that His perspective is 100 percent accurate, and His answers are always based on His infallible nature.

An example of this is found in the book of Luke where the Gos-pel writer tells about an elderly Jewish man named Simeon. Simeon waited for the arrival of the promised Messiah for years and years. The Jewish people expected a mighty military and political savior, a powerful king who would bring an end to the agony they suffered at the hands of the Roman government.

Read Luke 2:25-32 (page 781).
At the urging of the Holy Spirit, Simeon went to the temple expecting to see the rescuer of his people. Who did he find?

CHAPTER 7 | THE WEAPON

Put yourself in Simeon's place for a moment. For years you've been praying for rescue from the Romans. For years you've prayed for the arrival of the Messiah. At long last, you awake one morning knowing this is the day you get to see the answer to your prayers — the Messiah has arrived. Imagine the excitement you feel as you dress and depart for the temple. Imagine your pounding heart as you step through the door and scan the crowd anxious to catch a glimpse of the Messiah — your Rescuer — for whom you've prayed for so long. But you see no king in royal attire, no mighty warrior in full armor. All you see is a very young couple holding a tiny infant.

What would you have done next?

So often God's answers to prayer are not what we expect, are they? The Bible tells us His ways are higher than our ways and His thoughts higher than our thoughts (Isaiah 55:9, page 560). Because Simeon was not bound by his own expectations, he instantly recognized the baby Jesus as the long-awaited Messiah. That's what happens when you prayerfully develop your relationship with God — you recognize and trust God's answers. Praying increases hope and removes despair. It helps you let go of your limited perspective and stake your life on God's perspective instead.

Did you notice how Simeon referred to the Messiah in Luke 2:32 (page 781)? — A light

Light! The light that reveals God to the world. The light that illumi-
nates everything so our vision, our recognition, our ability to follow
Him becomes clear and accurate.

> What does the last part of Ephesians 6:18 (page 898) tell us to do?
>
> Pray in the Spirit

Be alert and persistent in our prayers for each other, recognizing
the battles we face, and supporting each other through continual
prayer. We need to stand firm, clothed in our armor, so united we
can ward off the darkness of this world and help our neighbors know
the Good News, stay strong, and participate in bringing God's light
to our world.

> After encouraging the Ephesians to pray for all believers, Paul specif-
> ically asks them to pray for him. What does he ask them to pray for
> in Ephesians 6:19-20 (page 898)?
>
> boldly

If you've ever felt uncomfortable sharing your faith, you are in good company! Even Paul felt that way — so much so that twice he asked them to pray for boldness as well as for the right words. Paul provides us a wonderful example. We should pray for our fellow Christians around the world as well as for ourselves — for boldness and the right words to share the Good News of the Gospel of Jesus Christ.

The book of Ephesians comes to a close with one final prayer from Paul.

Read Ephesians 6:23-24 (page 898).

The Message paraphrase says it this way: "Good-bye, friends. Love mixed with faith be yours from God the Father and from the Master, Jesus Christ. Pure grace and nothing but grace be with all who love our Master, Jesus Christ." Go forth in boldness now, with the whole armor of God protecting you. Let the light of Jesus Christ shine through you with ever increasing brilliance.

Closing Prayer

Lord, as I seek to follow You in all ways, may I put on every piece of Your armor so that I will be able to resist the enemy. Teach me to pray at all times and on every occasion, staying alert and persistent. Thank You for loving me and adopting me into your family and bringing me to you through Your Son, Jesus Christ. Let my heart always be flooded with Your light as I understand the incredible greatness of Your power within me. I give all praise to You for the grace and kindness You shower on me daily (Ephesians 6:13, 18, page 898; Ephesians 1:4, 6, 8, 18, 19, page 895).

Personal Reflection and Application

I see

I believe

I will

Thoughts, Notes, and Prayer Requests

GOD'S PURSUING LOVE

We can expect God to give us opportunities to share the gospel as we pray for our neighbors. This final section provides a sample guideline for what you might share in those conversations:

God, who created the universe, is full of love and mercy. He desires for you to personally receive His love and mercy.

It does not matter what has happened in your past. No matter what you've done, no matter what you regret about how you've lived your life, God's mercy is greater. God understands you — your hopes, your dreams, your frustrations, your loneliness, your heartaches. His love caused Him to pursue us, to leave heaven and come to Earth.

> For God so loved the world that he gave his one and only Son, that whoever believes in him shall not perish but have eternal life. For God did not send his Son into the world to condemn the world, but to save the world through him.
>
> –John 3:16-17

God is love. He is a God of relationship.

God created us to have a real and personal relationship with Him. Sin keeps us from having a loving relationship with God. We have all sinned and been separated from God. We all carry sin's consequences in our lives.

But God the Father loves so deeply that He made a way to close the gap of separation. He sent His Son Jesus to come to earth and live a perfect life with no sin and then to die in our place to take the punishment for our sin. Jesus Christ is God and He did the work for us.

Nothing we can do will earn us God's love. No good works. No good deeds. No avoidance of evil. "For God made Christ, who never sinned, to be the offering for our sin, so that we could be made right with God through Christ" (2 Corinthians 5:21).

> But God is so rich in mercy, and he loved us so much, that even though we were dead because of our sins, he gave us life when he raised Christ from the dead. (It is only by God's grace that you have been saved!)
>
> – Ephesians 2:4-5

Jesus Christ paid the penalty for sin when He died on the cross. But He did not stay dead! He came back to life. He rose from the dead. And He is ready to share His life with you.

Jesus is alive today.

He offers reconciliation to us. He can give you a new beginning and a newly created life. "This means that anyone who belongs in Christ has become a new person. The old life is gone; a new life has begun!" (2 Corinthians 5:17).

How do you begin this new life? Place your trust in Jesus Christ. Believe that He is God and receive the love He has for you. Agree with God about your sin and believe that Jesus came to close the separation between you and God. Ask Jesus to lead your life.

When you trust Jesus Christ, He will live in your life. God's Spirit will live inside you. The Holy Spirit will help you live a life that honors Him.

Would you like to begin this new life? You can start today with a few simple words like, "Dear Jesus, I believe that You are God and that You love me and came to save me through Your death and resurrection."

Or you might pray something like this:

> *Jesus, I believe you are the Son of God and that You died on the cross to pay the penalty for my sin. Forgive me. I choose to turn away from my sin and live a life that honors You. I want to follow You and make You the leader of my life. Thank You for Your gift of eternal life and for the Holy Spirit who has now come to live in me. Amen.*

When a woman in your group begins a relationship with Jesus Christ, Stonecroft would like to offer her a free download of *A New Beginning*, a short Bible study that will help her get started on her new faith journey. Please visit stonecroft.org/new beginning. You may also want to make sure she has a Bible. We recommend the New Living Translation (NLT). May God move mightily in response to your prayers!

Who is Stonecroft?

Every day Stonecroft communicates the gospel in meaningful ways. Whether side-by-side with a neighbor or new friend, or through a speaker sharing her transformational story, the Gospel of Jesus Christ goes forward. Through a variety of outreach activities and small group Bible studies specifically designed for those not familiar with God, and with online and print resources focused on evangelism, Stonecroft proclaims the love of Jesus Christ to women where they are, as they are.

For more than 75 years, Stonecroft volunteers have found ways to introduce women to Jesus Christ and train them to share His Good News with others — always with a foundation of prayer and reliance on God.

Stonecroft understands and appreciates the influence of one woman's life. When you reach her, you touch everyone she knows — her family, friends, neighbors, and co-workers. The real truth of the Gospel brings real redemption into real lives.

Our life-changing, faith-building community resources include:

- STONECROFT BIBLE STUDIES

  We offer both topical and chapter-by-chapter studies. We designed Stonecroft studies for those in small groups to simply yet profoundly discover God's Word together.

- *CONVERSATIONS*

  These thought-provoking small group resources engage women in conversation on topics that matter. *Conversations* include *Rest*, *Known*, and *Enough*.

- STONECROFT PRAYS

   This tool helps small groups of women pray for God to show them avenues to reach women in their community with the Gospel.

- OUTREACH EVENTS

   These set the stage for women to hear and share the gospel with their communities. Whether in a large venue, workshop, or small group setting, Stonecroft women find ways to share the love of Christ.

- STONECROFT MILITARY

   This specialized effort honors women connected to the U.S. military and shares with them the gospel while showing them the love of Christ.

- STONECROFT AWARE SERIES

   These resources reveal God's heart for those who do not yet know Him. The Aware Series includes *Aware*, *Belong*, and *Call*.

- STONECROFT.ORG

   Our site offers fresh content daily to equip and encourage you.

Dedicated and enthusiastic Stonecroft staff and volunteers serve together to engage women in sharing the love of Christ with the world. Your life matters. Join us today to become part of reaching your communities with the Gospel of Jesus Christ. Become involved with Stonecroft.

Resources

Discovering the Joy of Jesus
This study of Philippians helps you find
joy, regardless of your circumstances.
9 chapters

You Are Alive in Christ
Explore Colossians and discover our
intimate relationship with Christ.
8 chapters

God's Love Through You
The book of 1 John begins and ends talking
about a fulfilling, meaningful life.
9 chapters

Rest
This conversation helps you discover how God
enables us to find rest in an overly busy world.
4 Conversations

Known
Achievements and appearance don't determine real
worth, instead find love and acceptance in God's eyes.
4 Conversations

Enough
God helps us embrace who we really are,
rather than fear what we're missing.
4 Conversations

Endnotes

Chapter 1: Power for Those Who Believe

1 James Montgomery Boice, *Ephesians* (Grand Rapids, MI: Baker Books, 1997), 238.

2 Rick Renner, *Dressed to Kill* (Tulsa, OK: Harrison House, 1991), 374-375.

3 William Gurnell, *The Christian in Complete Armor, Volume 2* (Avon, Great Britian: Banner of Truth Trust, 1662-1665, reprinted in 1995), 134-161.

Chapter 2: Reconciled through Christ

1 Rick Renner, *Dressed to Kill* (Tulsa, OK: Harrison House, 1991), 292-294.

Chapter 3: Bold Faith

1 Kirsten Powers, "Fox News' Highly Reluctant Jesus Follower," *Christianity Today,* October 22, 2013, accessed May 16, 2015, http://www.christianitytoday.com/ct/2013/november/fox-news-highly-re-luctant-jesus-follower-kirsten-powers.html.

2 Rick Renner, *Dressed to Kill* (Tulsa, OK: Harrison House, 1991), 347-349.

3 Ibid., 351.

Chapter 4: The Value of Unity

[1] Rick Renner, *Dressed to Kill* (Tulsa, OK: Harrison House, 1991), 261-262.

Chapter 5: Living in the Light

[1] Rick Renner, *Dressed to Kill* (Tulsa, OK: Harrison House, 1991), 405-406.

[1] John Piper, *Ask Pastor John*, "If I'm Dead to Sin, Why Must I Kill It Every Day?" August 22, 2016, http://desiringgod.org.

[3] Billy Sunday, *Billy Sunday Quotes*, December 19, 2016, AZquotes.com.

Chapter 6: Finding Peace on Holy Ground

[1] Rick Renner, *Dressed to Kill* (Tulsa, OK: Harrison House, 1991), 313-314.

[2] Jon Courson, *Application Commentary* (Nashville, TN: Thomas Nelson Publishers, 2003), 1261.

[3] Rick Renner, *Dressed to Kill* (Tulsa, OK: Harrison House, 1991), 318.

Chapter 7: The Weapon

[1] Rick Renner, *Dressed to Kill* (Tulsa, OK: Harrison House, 1991), 437-439.

[2] Rick Renner, *Dressed to Kill* (Tulsa, OK: Harrison House, 1991), 444, 448.

[3] Jon Courson, *Application Commentary* (Nashville, TN: Thomas Nelson Publishers, 2003), 1269.